DONOVAN MCNABB, STEVE VAN BUREN, KEITH BYARS, HAROLD CARMICHAEL, TOMMY MCDONALD, PETE PIHOS, JON RUNYAN, BOB BROWN, WADE KEY, SHAWN ANDREWS, CHUCK BEDNARIK, REGGIE WHITE, CLYDE SIMMONS, CHARLIE JOHNSON, JEROME BROWN, SETH JOYNER, ALEX WOJCIECHOWICZ, ERIC ALLEN, TROY VINCENT, BRIAN DAWKINS, ANDRE WATERS, DAVID AKERS, SEAN LANDETA, DONOVAN MCNABB, STEVE VAN BUREN, KEITH BYARS, HAROLD CARMICHAEL, TOMMY MCDONALD, PETE PIHOS, JON

THE STORY OF THE PHILADELPHIA EAGLES

THE STORY OF THE
PHILADELPHIA EAGLES

BY JIM WHITING
CREATIVE EDUCATION / CREATIVE PAPERBACKS

PUBLISHED BY CREATIVE EDUCATION AND CREATIVE PAPERBACKS
P.O. BOX 227, MANKATO, MINNESOTA 56002
CREATIVE EDUCATION AND CREATIVE PAPERBACKS ARE IMPRINTS OF THE
CREATIVE COMPANY
WWW.THECREATIVECOMPANY.US

DESIGN AND PRODUCTION BY BLUE DESIGN (WWW.BLUEDES.COM)
ART DIRECTION BY RITA MARSHALL
PRINTED IN CHINA

PHOTOGRAPHS BY AP IMAGES (AP IMAGES, ASSOCIATED PRESS), CORBIS
(BETTMANN), GETTY IMAGES (GAVIN BAKER/ICON SPORTSWIRE, VERNON
BIEVER/NFL PHOTOS, STEPHEN DUNN, ELSA, FOCUS ON SPORT, GEORGE
GOJKOVICH, DREW HALLOWELL, HAROLD M. LAMBERT/LAMBERT, HUNTER
MARTIN, HUNTER MARTIN/NFL, HUNTER MARTIN/PHILADELPHIA EAGLES,
PATRICK MCDERMOTT, JOHN MCDONNELL/THE WASHINGTON POST, RONALD C.
MODRA/SPORTS IMAGERY, NFL, DOUG PENSINGER, STACY REVERE, ROBERT
RIGER, RICH SCHULTZ, GREGORY SHAMUS, PATRICK SMITH/STRINGER, VIC
STEIN/NFL, THOMAS E. WITTE)

NAMES: WHITING, JIM, AUTHOR.
TITLE: THE STORY OF THE PHILADELPHIA EAGLES / JIM WHITING.
SERIES: NFL TODAY.
INCLUDES INDEX.
SUMMARY: THIS HIGH-INTEREST HISTORY OF THE NATIONAL FOOTBALL
LEAGUE'S PHILADELPHIA EAGLES HIGHLIGHTS MEMORABLE GAMES,
SUMMARIZES SEASONAL TRIUMPHS AND DEFEATS, AND FEATURES STANDOUT
PLAYERS SUCH AS DONOVAN MCNABB.
IDENTIFIERS: LCCN 2018059140 / ISBN 978-1-64026-155-6 (HARDCOVER) / ISBN
978-1-62832-718-2 (PBK) / ISBN 978-1-64000-273-9 (EBOOK)
SUBJECTS: LCSH: PHILADELPHIA EAGLES (FOOTBALL TEAM)—HISTORY—
JUVENILE LITERATURE. / PHILADELPHIA EAGLES (FOOTBALL TEAM)—
HISTORY.
CLASSIFICATION: LCC GV956.P44 W55 2019 / DDC 796.332/640974811—DC23

FIRST EDITION HC 9 8 7 6 5 4 3 2 1
FIRST EDITION PBK 9 8 7 6 5 4 3 2 1

COVER: CARSON WENTZ
PAGE 2: ZACH ERTZ
PAGES 6–7: KURT COLEMAN AND JASON BABIN

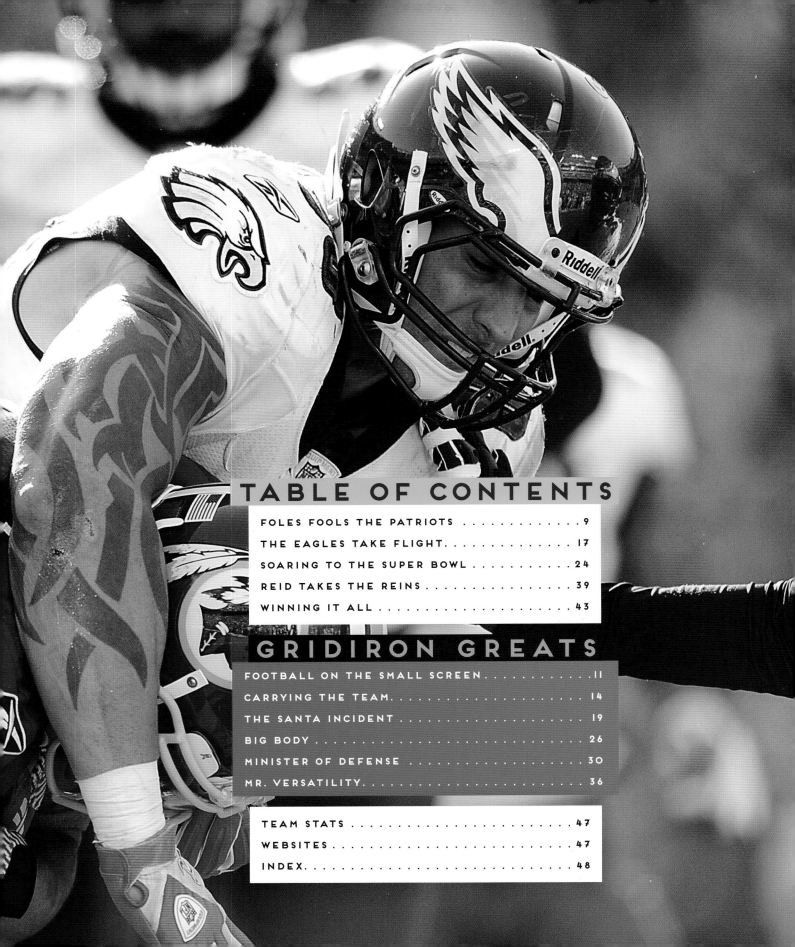

TABLE OF CONTENTS

GRIDIRON GREATS

FOLES FOOLS
THE PATRIOTS

Less than a minute remained in the first half of Super Bowl LII. The Philadelphia Eagles clung to a 15–12 lead over the New England Patriots. They had the ball on New England's one-yard line. It was fourth down. But the Eagles decided not to kick a field goal. Quarterback Nick Foles lined up in the shotgun formation. Rookie running back Corey Clement was behind him. Foles stepped aside. Clement took the snap. He rolled out to his left. Then he pitched the ball to tight end Trey Burton. Burton circled back to his right. Meanwhile, Foles drifted into the end zone. The Patriots' defense ignored him. Burton threw the ball to Foles. It was an easy touchdown. The trick play was called the "Philly Special."

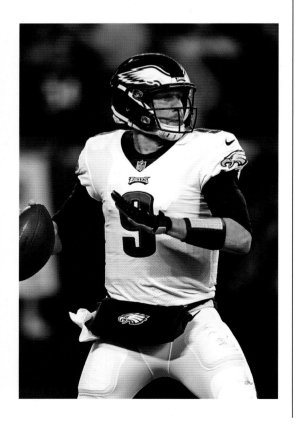

It was one of the keys to the Eagles' 41–33 Super Bowl victory. It was their first National Football League (NFL) championship in 57 years.

"That's just something we've been working on," Foles said after the game. "I was like, 'Let's just run it.' It was a good time, and the end was a little wider than I thought, so I was like, 'I really need to sell like I'm not doing anything.' And it worked." The Patriots had tried a similar play earlier in the game. But quarterback Tom Brady did not make the catch.

Foles was an unlikely hero. He had come off the bench for starting quarterback Carson Wentz. Wentz had suffered a season-ending knee injury. Many experts thought that doomed Philadelphia's Super Bowl chances. The team struggled to win two of its three remaining regular season games. The Dallas Cowboys shut it out 6–0 in the final game. It nearly lost to the Atlanta Falcons in

GRIDIRON GREATS ∨
FOOTBALL ON THE SMALL SCREEN

The Philadelphia Eagles played in the first televised NFL game. It was held on October 22, 1939. They faced the Brooklyn Dodgers. NBC broadcast the game to approximately 500 televisions in the New York City area. The broadcast didn't have any commercials. But there were other interruptions. It was a cloudy day. The cameras needed lots of light. Sometimes the clouds blocked the sun. The picture would go blank. When that happened, the broadcast team would simply switch to a radio. Then the clouds would pass. There was enough light again. The Eagles lost the game, 23–14. But they earned a special place in NFL broadcasting history.

THE "PHILLY SPECIAL"

"THAT'S JUST SOMETHING WE'VE BEEN WORKING ON."

the first round of the playoffs. Kicker Jake Elliot booted two field goals in the second half to secure the 15–10 win.

Foles came alive in the National Football Conference (NFC) Championship Game. The Eagles faced the Minnesota Vikings. Foles became the second Eagles quarterback to throw for more than 300 yards and 3 touchdowns in the postseason. Philadelphia soared to a 38–7 victory. Foles carried that momentum into the Super Bowl. He threw for 373 yards and 3 touchdowns. He became the first player in Super Bowl history to both throw a touchdown pass and catch one. He was named the game's Most Valuable Player (MVP).

ELPHIA EAGLES

STEVE VAN BUREN
HALFBACK

EAGLES SEASONS: 1944–51
HEIGHT: 6 FEET
WEIGHT: 200 POUNDS

GRIDIRON GREATS v
CARRYING THE TEAM

The Eagles selected Steve Van Buren with the fifth overall pick in the 1944 NFL Draft. In 1945, he achieved a remarkable "triple crown." He led the league in rushing yards, kickoff return touchdowns, and points scored. One of his most memorable performances came in the 1949 NFL championship. He carried the ball 31 times for 196 yards. The Eagles beat the Los Angeles Rams, 14–0. Teammate Chuck Bednarik said, "[Van Buren] just put us on his shoulders and absolutely ran wild on that day." When Van Buren retired, he was the NFL's all-time leading rusher with 5,860 yards.

72

83

83 GAMES PLAYED

15

THE EAGLES TAKE FLIGHT

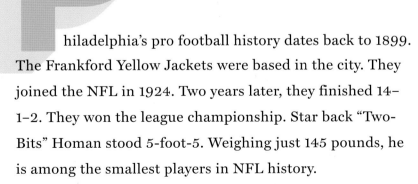

Philadelphia's pro football history dates back to 1899. The Frankford Yellow Jackets were based in the city. They joined the NFL in 1924. Two years later, they finished 14–1–2. They won the league championship. Star back "Two-Bits" Homan stood 5-foot-5. Weighing just 145 pounds, he is among the smallest players in NFL history.

The Yellow Jackets went bankrupt before the 1931 season. Two years later, former college teammates Bert Bell and Lud Wray bought the rights to field a new team in Philadelphia. They named their franchise the Eagles. The birds symbolize American freedom. They are a fitting

11

11 LOSSES TO START THE 1968 SEASON

29

29 INTERCEPTIONS THROWN IN 1968

GRIDIRON GREATS v
THE SANTA INCIDENT

On December 15, 1968, the Eagles scheduled a halftime Christmas pageant. It would include a visit from Santa. But there was too much snow on the field. The pageant was canceled. Instead, the team hired fan Frank Olivo to run around the field. He had worn a Santa suit to the game. At that time, the Eagles had posted losing records for several seasons. Fans were angry with team management. They took out their frustration on Olivo. They booed. They pelted him with snowballs. Olivo escaped unharmed. "I thought it was funny," he said afterward.

PHILADELPHIA EAGLES

COACH GREASY NEALE

mascot for Philadelphia. The United States Declaration of Independence was signed there. It took time for the fledgling Eagles to take flight. Between 1933 and 1942, they won just 23 games. In three of those seasons, they had just a single victory.

Millions of young men went overseas to fight in World War II in the early 1940s. The NFL suffered a shortage of players. For the 1943 season, the Eagles merged with the Pittsburgh Steelers. They were called the "Steagles." They posted a 5–4–1 record. It was Philadelphia's first winning season. Afterward, the merger ended.

The Eagles picked halfback Steve Van Buren in the 1944 NFL Draft. He helped the team soar. It finished at 7–1–2. By 1947, Philadelphia was in the playoffs. It fell to the Chicago Cardinals in the NFL Championship Game. But the Eagles stormed back the following year. They went 9–2–1. Once again, they faced Chicago for the NFL title. The field was covered with snow. In the fourth quarter, Van Buren powered into the end zone. It was the only score of the game. The Eagles won their first NFL championship.

The next season, the team won 11 games. It returned to the NFL Championship Game. This time, it played the Los Angeles Rams. The field was wet and muddy. The Eagles blanked the Rams, 14–0.

After that, Philadelphia stumbled. The Eagles limped through the 1950s. They failed to make the playoffs. One constant of those teams was Chuck Bednarik. The Eagles had made him the top overall draft pick in 1949. They quickly realized that he was far too valuable to sit on

END PETE PIHOS (NUMBER 35)

PHILADELPHIA EAGLES

IN THE OFF-SEASON, BEDNARIK SOLD CONCRETE. A LOCAL SPORTSWRITER SAID HE WAS "AS HARD AS THE CONCRETE HE SELLS."

the sidelines. They made him the starting linebacker on defense. By his second season, he was also the starting center on offense. His nickname was the "60-Minute Man." In the off-season, Bednarik sold concrete. A local sportswriter said he was "as hard as the concrete he sells." He missed only 3 games in 14 NFL seasons.

In 1958, Philadelphia added veteran quarterback Norm Van Brocklin. He embraced his role as a leader on the field. His passing arm carried the Eagles to an improved 7–5 mark in 1959. In 1960, the team rolled to 10–2. Van Brocklin was named the league's MVP. Philadelphia met the Green Bay Packers in the NFL championship. It was a hard-fought contest. The Eagles trailed by three in the fourth quarter. Van Brocklin engineered a touchdown drive. Then Bednarik made a last-minute tackle to lock in the Eagles' 17–13 victory.

SOARING TO THE SUPER BOWL

During the next 17 seasons, the team had just 2 winning records. Still, there were a few highlights. In 1972, wide receiver Harold Jackson topped the league. He had 62 receptions for 1,048 yards. The next year, towering young receiver Harold Carmichael led the league with 67 catches. Despite these performances, the Eagles continued to sputter.

In 1976, Dick Vermeil was named head coach. He worked tirelessly to turn the Eagles around. He often slept in his office instead of going home. In 1978, his efforts paid off. The Eagles went 9–7. They returned to the playoffs

GRIDIRON GREATS v
BIG BODY

Quarterbacks love a big target. Harold Carmichael created matchup problems for defenses. He remains one of the tallest receivers in NFL history. He had rare leaping ability, too. Eagles quarterbacks only needed to throw the ball up high. Carmichael would go up and snatch it out of the air above the defenders' heads. He was also durable. He played in 162 straight games for the Eagles. He still holds franchise records for touchdowns (79), receiving yards (8,978), and receptions (589). "He was the first big receiver in the NFL," said Alva Tabor Jr., who coached Carmichael at Louisiana's Southern University and A&M College. "Harold actually changed the game."

79

79 CAREER TOUCHDOWNS

182

182 GAMES PLAYED

for four straight seasons. Carmichael, quarterback Ron Jaworski, and running back Wilbert Montgomery were key players.

In 1980, the Eagles topped the NFC East Division. They finished at 12–4. Philly fans cheered. The team flew by the Vikings and the Cowboys in the playoffs. It landed in Super Bowl XV. It faced the Raiders. Oakland beat Philadelphia, 27–10. Still, the Eagles held their heads high. "Four years ago, this team was a doormat," said Jaworski. "Now we're Super Bowl material. You know how satisfying that is?"

Following the 1982 season, Vermeil resigned. He had guided the Eagles to newfound respectability. After he left, the Eagles struggled. They clearly needed something big. In 1984, they got it. They drafted Reggie White, a 6-foot-5 and 291-pound defensive end. He had 13 sacks in his rookie year. Philadelphia hoped to build a mighty defense. It hired Buddy Ryan as head coach in 1986. He had been the defensive coordinator for the Chicago Bears. In 1987,

MINISTER OF DEFENSE

Reggie White began preaching at his Baptist church at age 17. He became an ordained minister. In the NFL, he was nicknamed "The Minister of Defense." He had a passion for stopping opposing offenses. Year after year, he put up double-digit sack totals. He was selected to 13 straight Pro Bowls. In 1987, White enjoyed one of the best years by any defensive lineman in history. The season was shortened by a strike. There were just 12 games. Yet he finished with a career-high 21 sacks. His Philadelphia career ended in 1992. At that time, he was the only player in NFL history to have more sacks (124) than games played (121).

REGGIE WHITE
DEFENSIVE END

EAGLES SEASONS: 1985–92
HEIGHT: 6-FOOT-5
WEIGHT: 291 POUNDS

PHILADELPHIA EAGLES

Randall Cunningham took over as starting quarterback. He could sprint like a wide receiver. He had a strong arm, too.

With Cunningham at the helm, the team began to soar. In 1988, he and rookie tight end Keith Jackson led the Eagles to 10–6. They made the playoffs. Unfortunately, in the second half of the game, the field became shrouded in mist. The Eagles fell prey to the Bears. Today, that game is known as the "Fog Bowl."

RANDALL CUNNINGHAM

The next year, the Eagles stormed
to 11–5. The Rams knocked them out of the playoffs.
In 1990, Cunningham threw for 3,466 yards and 30
touchdowns. He also ran a whopping 942 yards. Despite
his performance, the Eagles lost the Wild Card for the
second year in a row. Ryan was fired.

Philadelphia returned to the playoffs in 1992. It ran
over the New Orleans Saints in the Wild Card game. But
the Cowboys blew the Eagles out of the playoffs in the
divisional round. Three years later, the Eagles won a playoff
blowout of their own. They crushed the Detroit Lions,
58–37. A week later, the Cowboys again overwhelmed
Philadelphia, 30–11. After that, the team began to slip. In
1998, the once-mighty Eagles went just 3–13.

GRIDIRON GREATS v
MR. VERSATILITY

Randall Cunningham was a superb all-around athlete. He had a strong arm and great speed. He also had the elusive moves of a running back. He became the starting quarterback in 1987. For the next four seasons, Cunningham was a prolific passer. He also led the Eagles in rushing. In 1989, he kicked a surprise 91-yard punt. It is one of the longest punts in NFL history. It helped the Eagles beat the New York Giants. His style of play paved the way for future fleet-footed quarterbacks such as Donovan McNabb and Russell Wilson.

161

161 GAMES PLAYED

242

242 CAREER TOUCHDOWNS

BRIAN DAWKINS

REID TAKES THE REINS

Andy Reid became head coach in 1999. His leadership sparked a resurgence. The Eagles improved their record by two games during Reid's first season. Then they shot to 11–5. The driving force behind this improvement was second-year quarterback Donovan McNabb. Fans had booed when the Eagles drafted him the previous season. "Donovan's a sharp kid," Reid said. "I know he'll turn into a top-notch quarterback." Sure enough, people soon began comparing him to Cunningham. In 2000, McNabb threw for 3,365 yards. He rushed for 629 more.

Philadelphia was tough on the other side of the ball, too. Defensive end Hugh Douglas was a pass-rushing expert. Cornerback Troy Vincent and safety Brian Dawkins led an aggressive secondary. The Eagles stifled the

COACH ANDY REID

Tampa Bay Buccaneers, 21–3, in a playoff victory. It was Philadelphia's first playoff win in five years.

The team continued to improve. It advanced to the NFC Championship Game for the next two seasons. But it lost both times. Philadelphia did even better in 2003. Versatile running back Brian Westbrook led the team in touchdowns. He also returned punts and kickoffs. Philadelphia defeated Green Bay to reach the NFC Championship Game. Once again, the Eagles came up just short of the Super Bowl. The Carolina Panthers beat them, 14–3.

Philadelphia bolstered its roster in the off-season. One addition was defensive end Jevon Kearse. He was nicknamed "The Freak." He relentlessly pursued quarterbacks. The team also signed wide receiver Terrell Owens. He was big and fast. He was known for his talent and over-the-top ego. The Eagles came out swinging in 2004. Owens amassed 14 touchdowns and 1,200 receiving yards. The team flew to 13–3. It was the best record in franchise history. In the playoffs, the Eagles overwhelmed the Vikings and the Falcons. They faced the Patriots in Super Bowl XXXIX. It was a close game. But Philadelphia committed four turnovers. It was too many to overcome. New England won, 24–21. The Eagles went home empty-handed.

McNabb suffered nagging injuries in 2005. Philadelphia plummeted to 6–10. The 2006 Eagles reached the playoffs. But the Saints knocked them out in the divisional round. They missed the postseason in 2007.

Philadelphia had nine wins the following year. They

sneaked into the playoffs. Despite their modest record, the Eagles rallied in the postseason. They defeated the Vikings and the New York Giants. They reached the conference championship for the fifth time in eight years. Philadelphia rallied for a late 25–24 lead over Arizona. But the Cardinals drove for the game-winning touchdown. They squashed Philly's hopes of a return to the Super Bowl.

DONOVAN MCNABB

WINNING IT ALL

Many had grown weary of the team's near misses. Before the 2009 season, the franchise made a controversial decision. It signed quarterback Michael Vick. Many fans were upset by the move. Vick had previously been involved in a dogfighting ring. He had spent two years in prison. During the season, Vick played sparingly. McNabb led the Eagles to 11–5. Unfortunately, they lost in the Wild Card. The team traded McNabb.

Vick became a starter in 2010. He shocked the NFL with the best season of his career. He demonstrated a new poise and leadership. He was named the NFL's Comeback Player of the Year. The Eagles finished 10–6. They lost in the first round of the playoffs. But the future looked bright.

DESEAN JACKSON

The Eagles added several talented defensive players. Cornerback Nnamdi Asomugha joined two lightning-quick scoring threats: Running back LeSean McCoy and receiver DeSean Jackson were coming into their prime. Unfortunately, individual talent did not translate into team success. The Eagles struggled early in 2011. They finished with a four-game winning streak. But it was too late. With just eight wins, Philadelphia missed the playoffs. The team dropped to 4–12 the following season. Despite his impressive record, Reid was fired.

The Eagles returned to the playoffs in 2013. On the final play of the Wild Card game, the Saints kicked a field goal. They beat Philadelphia, 26–24. In 2014, the Eagles' 10–6 record was not good enough for the playoffs. Nor were their 7–9 records in the following two seasons. Philadelphia picked Carson Wentz second overall in the 2016 Draft. That season, he completed 379 passes. It was an NFL rookie record. He gave fans hope for the future.

Wentz was even better in 2017. By mid-season, some people thought he might be named MVP. That would be remarkable feat for a second-year player. But a December knee injury put him out for the season. The team turned to its backup, Nick Foles. He had been Philadelphia's starter in late 2013 and early 2014. Then he was injured. The Eagles traded him. He signed with them again in 2017. When Wentz was injured, many doubted whether the team would be able to continue its performance. Questioned by reporters, safety Malcolm Jenkins responded, "Do we have a quarterback on the roster?" They nodded. "Okay, then,

LESEAN MCCOY

DEFENSIVE END FLETCHER COX

yes," he said. The Eagles went on to win their first Super Bowl. The next year followed the same pattern: Wentz was injured late in the season, and Foles resumed his lead. After narrowly beating the Bears in the Wild Card, the Eagles faced the Saints in the playoffs. Philadelphia stalled as the Saints marched to victory.

The historic city of Philadelphia has long been a site of resilience. The Eagles have embodied that attitude on the gridiron. From powerful Steve Van Buren and Chuck Bednarik to the dominant Reggie White and the hard-nosed Donovan McNabb, Philadelphia players have always been tough. Today's young and talented Eagles continue to soar in the highest levels of the NFL.

NFL CHAMPIONSHIPS

1948, 1949, 1960, 2017

WEBSITES

PHILADELPHIA EAGLES

https://www.philadelphiaeagles.com/

NFL: PHILADELPHIA EAGLES TEAM PAGE

http://www.nfl.com/teams/philadelphiaeagles/profile?team=PHI

INDEX

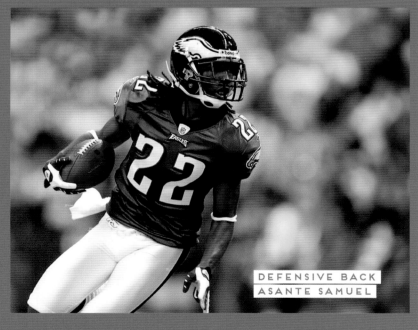

DEFENSIVE BACK
ASANTE SAMUEL